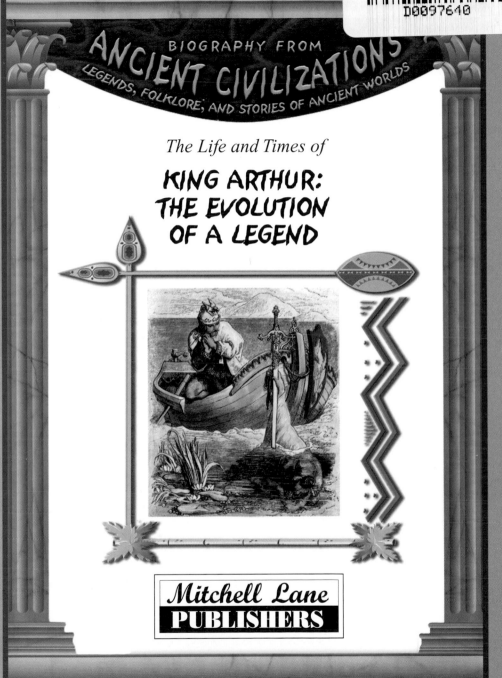

BIOGRAPHY FROM ANCIENT CIVILIZATIONS

LEGENDS, FOLKLORE, AND STORIES OF ANCIENT WORLDS

The Life and Times of

KING ARTHUR: THE EVOLUTION OF A LEGEND

Mitchell Lane
PUBLISHERS

P.O. Box 196
Hockessin, Delaware 19707

Titles in the Series

The Life and Times of:

BIOGRAPHY FROM
ANCIENT CIVILIZATIONS
LEGENDS, FOLKLORE, AND STORIES OF ANCIENT WORLDS

The Life and Times of

KING ARTHUR: THE EVOLUTION OF A LEGEND

Susan Sales Harkins
and William H. Harkins

Printing   1   2   3   4   5   6   7   8   9

Library of Congress Cataloging-in-Publication Data

Harkins, Susan Sales.
      Legend of King Arthur/by Susan Sales Harkins and William H. Harkins.
            p. cm.—(Biography from ancient civilizations)
      Includes bibliographical references and index.
      ISBN 1-58415-513-2 (lib. bdg.)
1. Arthur, King—Juvenile literature. 2. Britons—Kings and rulers—Juvenile literature.
3. Great Britain—History—To 1066—Juvenile literature. 4. Great Britain—Antiquities,
Celtic—Juvenile literature. 5. Arthurian romances—Juvenile literature. I. Harkins, William H.
II. Title. III. Series.
DA152.5A7H37 2007
942.01'4—dc22
                                                                                          2006006103
ISBN-10: 1-58415-513-2   ISBN-13: 9781584155133

ABOUT THE AUTHORS: Susan and Bill Harkins live in Kentucky, where they enjoy writing together for children. Susan has written many books for adults and children. Bill is a history buff. In addition to writing, Bill is a member of the Kentucky Civil Air Patrol, where he helps Kentuckians prepare for natural disasters.

PHOTO CREDITS: Cover—North Wind Picture Archives; p. 6—Corbis; p. 10—Getty Images; p. 13—Andrea Pickens; p. 16—Superstock; p. 19—Corbis; p. 24—Getty Images; p. 26—North Wind Picture Archives; p. 27—Corbis; p. 30—North Wind Picture Archives; pp. 34, 37, 40—Corbis

PUBLISHER'S NOTE: This story is based on the authors' extensive research, which they believe to be accurate. Documentation of such research is contained on page 46.
      The internet sites referenced herein were active as of the publication date. Due to the fleeting nature of some web sites, we cannot guarantee they will all be active when you are reading this book.
      To reflect current usage, we have chosen to use the secular era designations BCE ("before the common era") and CE ("of the common era") instead of the traditional designations BC ("before Christ") and AD (*anno Domini*, "in the year of the Lord").

                                                                                                      PLB

BIOGRAPHY FROM

ANCIENT CIVILIZATIONS
LEGENDS, FOLKLORE, AND STORIES OF ANCIENT WORLDS

The Life and Times of

KING ARTHUR: THE EVOLUTION OF A LEGEND

Sir Bedivere comforts King Arthur as a mysterious boat approaches. Modred usually receives credit for killing King Arthur in a fierce and final battle between the two enemies. In later versions, the Lady of the Lake spirits the wounded king off to Avalon, where she heals his wounds.

CHAPTER
ONE

THE LEGEND AND THE MAN

King Arthur pulled his sword from the slain soldier. Quickly, he raised Excalibur to block the next attacker, but he met only air and silence. Still brandishing his sword, the good king looked about. Thousands of men lay dead or dying on the beach. How could so many men die so quickly? he wondered. He saw only two of his knights, Sir Lucan and Sir Bedivere, still standing. He could find none of his enemy's men still fighting. Then, off a distance among the dead, his eyes fell on his enemy—his son, Modred.

Leaping over the corpses, Modred ran at his father.

With Excalibur poised high above his head, King Arthur waited.

Their swords met in the air with a mighty clang! One of them must die.

While Modred had his fury, King Arthur had Excalibur. Anyone wielding the enchanted sword was promised to win in battle. Modred knew of the sword's power, but he was insane with hatred. In the evening shadows, the king watched his son's dark, tormented face register shock as Excalibur pierced Modred's heart.

Any other man would have dropped to his knees and died immediately. Driven by hatred for his father, Modred summoned all his strength and took one last breath. He reached for his father with one arm, as if to embrace him—but King Arthur received no dying embrace from his son that day. Instead, with his free hand, Modred thrust his sword into his father's side.

Modred fell to the ground, dead.

King Arthur also fell to the ground. Despite the easy victory, the wounded king was ready to die. He grieved for all he had lost. His beautiful wife, Guinevere, was lost to him forever, having betrayed him with his beloved knight, Sir Lancelot. Never again would he embrace either his wife or his son. Without the people he loved the most, he did not want to live.

He needed Merlin. Surely the wizard's magic was strong enough to turn back time. Sleeping the decades away in his cave, Merlin knew nothing of Arthur's troubles. Many times over the past few months, Arthur had cried out to Merlin, but his cries were never loud enough to wake the sleeping sorcerer. King Arthur was truly alone.

Exhausted and dying, King Arthur asked Bedivere to return Excalibur to the Lady of the Lake. She had given the sword to him years before, and it had to be returned to her now that he was dying. The sword was too powerful to be trusted to evil hands.

Bedivere wanted to obey his king. He stood by the water's edge and tried many times to throw the sword, but Excalibur was too beautiful and its magic too powerful. He hid the sword instead.

Arthur, knowing the sword's magical allure, asked Bedivere what he'd seen after he'd thrown the sword into the lake. The knight lied and replied that he'd seen nothing—only the lake blown by the wind. King Arthur knew Bedivere had failed. Near death, he again commanded Bedivere to throw Excalibur into the lake. Bedivere tried again, but failed.

King Arthur no longer had the strength to command Bedivere. Gasping for air, he sadly said that the future was lost to them. Moved by his king's grief, Bedivere finally threw Excalibur toward the middle of the lake.

As the sword flashed through the air, a woman's hand rose from the still water. Effortlessly, the Lady of the Lake caught the sword and brandished it three times.

Then Bedivere caught sight of a small boat rowing out of the lake's mist, carrying several women dressed in black. Once the boat reached the shore, Bedivere and Lucan placed King Arthur on board. Bedivere asked if Arthur would die. One of the women stood and removed her black hood. It was Nimue, the Lady of the Lake. She promised that King Arthur would never die and that someday he would return, for he was the once and future king.

The legend of King Arthur, some of which is retold above, bears some truth. Both the King Arthur of legend and the real man on whom the legend is most likely based were Britons. Both men were warriors who sought peace and died in battle. That is where the similarities end.

To tell the real Arthur's story, we must go back to a time when civilization was young, centuries before Arthur was born. It was a time when Britons lived as one with the forest and the rivers. During those days, warriors left their hiding places to plunder and kill. Those who lived returned to the dark forest at night, to hide once again from their enemies. The island was a savage place.

Other places in Europe were more civilized. One such place was Rome. In those days, Julius Caesar marched north through the continent, demanding loyalty from every village he passed. Few people were brave enough to challenge the Roman soldiers.

Romans were civilized, but they were also greedy. Europe wasn't enough of a conquest for them, so they sailed across the channel to the British Isles.

Centuries before Arthur's birth, the Roman armies of Julius Caesar invaded Britain and subdued the Celtic tribes. For several hundred years, the Romans kept the peace on the once savage island. When the Romans retreated, the Britons were once again at the mercy of the violent Picts and Saxons.

When the Romans arrived, Britain changed forever—some say for the better. The Romans lived well. They built roads and imported exotic foods from faraway places. They built forts and protected the Britons from the Picts and the Welsh. Most profoundly, the Romans shared the news of Jesus, whom they considered their Christ, or Savior.

Britons traded their bows for farm tools. They washed their bodies clean of war paints. They preferred Roman togas to their old animal skins. Eventually, Rome and Britain allied against the Welsh, the Cornwalls, and the Picts.

Then the seemingly impossible happened. In August of 410 CE, an army of barbarians, known as the Visigoths, sacked faraway Rome. Other tribes took advantage of the opportunity to attack Roman territories throughout Europe. Rome's empire began to crumble.

Under attack, Rome sent the word throughout Europe and even across the channel into Britain—Romans come home! Soldiers and nobles alike fled their remote outposts and made their way back to Rome. By 450 CE, most Romans had fled Britain. Only a few, including some nobles, stayed behind. Although they were Roman by blood and ancestry, their families had lived on the island for generations. Britain, not Rome, was their home.

Without Roman soldiers to protect them, the Britons were defenseless. Once again, they were at the mercy of the Picts and Welsh. Without Rome's strong leadership, the Britons returned to their tribal ways. Warlords filled the void that the Romans left when they abandoned the island. The warlords fought one another for the right to rule all of Britain. Civil war ripped apart the land and its people.

Caught between powers greater than themselves, the common people suffered. Every village was at the mercy of cruel warlords and their armed men, who roamed the forests and moors. For the next forty years, Britain was a terrifying place to live. The Roman estates and baths fell into decay as nature reclaimed the land. The country fell into lawlessness.

The situation got worse when the Saxons invaded. Saxon, Anglo, and Jute warriors from the mainland combined forces. They sailed across the North Sea and attacked the island. Once on shore, the low *thumb! . . . thumb! . . . thumb! . . .* of the Saxon drums rumbled ahead of their large armies, striking terror in even the bravest men. Saxons were ruthless. They killed everyone in their path, including women and children. They left no one behind who might someday wield a sword against them.

Even in the face of the savage Saxons, the British nobles fought for their way of life. They were wealthy and well educated, and they were still part of the glorious Roman Empire. They resisted the plundering Saxons.

About this time, a new warlord came to power. Instead of fighting the Saxons, Vortigern joined forces with them. The Saxons received land in southern Britain in return for fighting against the Picts with Vortigern. It was a grave mistake on Vortigern's part. Soon, the Saxons demanded more money and more land. Vortigern refused, and the Saxons attacked Britain from their southern settlements.

Into this savage world Arthur was born—into a Britain of chaos, greed, terror, and early graves. Saxons invaded from the north and the south, burning and killing their way inland. Picts and Welsh raided from the north and west.

Vortigern had failed. Britain needed a leader who was strong enough to unite the warlords against the Saxons, the Picts, and the Welsh.

None tried harder than Ambrosius Aurelianus, a Roman warrior who had remained in Britain when Rome recalled its citizens. Born and raised in Britain, Rome was just a dream to him. In Britain, his destiny was to become king; he could never rule Rome.

To succeed, he had to conquer all the other warlords. Eventually, that goal took him west to Cornwall. In battle, Aurelianus killed Gorlois, the Duke of Cornwall. Later, he married the duke's widow, Ygerna (or Igraine), to secure the peace between Cornwall and his British kingdom. Ygerna was beautiful, so his sacrifice for peace was small.

Ygerna had a young son named Arthur. Aurelianus adopted Arthur as his heir and treated him well. He raised his stepson as a Roman warrior.

Eventually, Aurelianus faced Vortigern in battle and was victorious. Like Vortigern, Aurelianus did not know peace long. The Saxons were still a plague on his island—no one could hide from them, and they showed no mercy in battle. With Vortigern out of the way, only the Saxons stood in Aurelianus' way to a united and peaceful Britain. Aurelianus killed the Saxon leader in battle. Still, the Saxons refused to leave his island.

Warring tribes from the north, west, and south attacked the Britons. Of these, the Saxons were the most ruthless, killing everyone in their path. The Picts and the Welsh attacked from their strongholds to the north and west, attacking villages without warning and then disappearing into the forest.

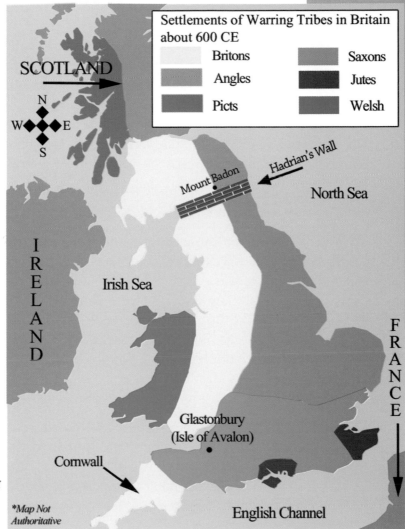

Settlements of Warring Tribes in Britain about 600 CE

Britons		Saxons	
Angles		Jutes	
Picts		Welsh	

SCOTLAND

N
W E
S

IRELAND

Irish Sea

Mount Badon

Hadrian's Wall

North Sea

FRANCE

Glastonbury
(Isle of Avalon)

Cornwall

Map Not Authoritative

English Channel

Arthur spent his boyhood on the battlefield. By the time Aurelianus clashed with the Saxons at Mount Badon, Arthur was second in command. He and his men camped at a small fortress along Hadrian's Wall, an ancient wall that at one time separated the civilized Britons from the barbaric Picts to the north.

The Saxons surrounded Arthur's men and cut off their supply route. Arthur's men were prepared for just such a siege. After several days of waiting, the Saxons finally left. Arthur wasn't willing to let the Saxons go in peace. He and his men followed the retreating army and caught them by surprise. The Battle of Mount Badon, which was fought sometime between 490 and 517 CE, was one of the bloodiest in all of British history. Not one Saxon was left alive. Arthur had finally broken the Saxon curse. The Saxons had fallen not to a king, not even to a prince, but to a warrior—to Arthur.

For the next forty years, Arthur's Britain lived in peace. Britons still call this prosperous time the Golden Age of Britain.

We'll probably never know the full and truthful story of Arthur, his life, his battles, his wives, his children, or even his death. We have only a few facts. There was a real Arthur. He was born about 470 CE to a Christian and noble family. They were Romans, or at least they lived peacefully with the Romans. As an adult, Arthur led a group of warriors in many battles against warlords and Celtic tribes (Welsh, Cornwall, and Picts). His defeat of the Saxons brought lasting peace to the island. Many years after driving the Saxons from the island, Arthur died in a civil war, most likely at the Battle of Camlann.

By 600 CE, the Saxons had returned and conquered most of Britain. Only Cornwall, Wales, and Scotland remained free of Saxon rule. Eventually, Britain became known as Angleland, after the Angles who fought with the Saxons. In time, *Angleland* evolved to *Angland* and then finally to *England*.

Over the next one thousand years, the Roman Arthur who united the Britons also evolved. He became the legendary King Arthur.

Fifth-Century Weapons

Most of the weapons used by Arthur and his men during the fifth century were of Roman design. Cavalrymen used long swords and metal shields. Many were skilled with a long spear. Infantrymen used a common short sword. Although some infantrymen preferred a battle-ax, they also carried metal shields and spears, and daggers and boot knives for close combat. For protection, they wore light chain mail, a metal breastplate, and a metal helmet.

Chain mail

Archers often carried a short sword and a dagger or foot knife. They also wore a light chain mail covering. Because they operated from behind the front line, archers wore leather breastplates and helmets. Wearing lighter gear, they could move quickly behind the main troops.

The Celtic tribes (Welsh, Cornwalls, and Picts) chose much lighter arms than the Romans and Britons. They seldom wore armor, but they did wear leather or animal skins, which offered some protection. Some were skilled with swords and spears of varying length, but all were experts with the bow and arrow. Celtic women fought alongside the men in battles. The Celts' main strength was the hit-and-run tactics they used. They wouldn't fight in the open if they could help it.

Before battle, the Picts covered themselves from head to toe with blue paint. Many covered their bodies with tattoos. With their long, wild hair flying, their blue skin, and dressed in animal hides, the Picts terrified their opponents.

Saxons, Angles, and Jutes were ruthless and relentless fighters. They combined metal armor, leather, and animal skins for protection. Their swords and spears varied in length. Many used the battle-ax. Their powerful crossbolts had a shorter range than the Celtic and British bow and arrows. The Saxon, Anglo, and Jute invaders posed such a horrific threat that the Picts and Welsh joined forces with the Britons in order to resist them.

Merlin the sorcerer serves as Arthur's mentor and adviser. Merlin enters the written legend during the ninth century, thanks to a Welsh monk named Nennius. Verbal traditions had included a magician for centuries.

CHAPTER
TWO

OUT OF THE DARK AGES

Some say that at the beginning of the Dark Ages, a bright object appeared in the skies over Britain. It was huge and so bright that people below could see it during the day as well as at night. A single ray lit the object's path across the sky. At the ray's point, a dragon danced while two beams of light poured from its mouth. One beam brilliantly lit the way to France. The second stretched to the Irish Sea, where it finally split into seven smaller beams.

Frightened Britons turned to Merlin, a magical but earthbound creature who was half man and half demon. The star and the dragon were Uther, the next king, Merlin explained. The southern beam was Uther's son, Arthur, who would unite and rule all the lands covered by the bright light. The second beam, which split into several more beams, were Arthur's children, who would rule Britain after him.

The legend of King Arthur came to light during the Dark Ages, but celestial bodies had nothing to do with it. The people needed the story. In the days following Arthur's death, Britons shared his story, from camp to camp, from father to son, and from warrior to warrior.

Most historians identify the years from around 476 CE to 1000 CE as the Dark Ages. Era-wise this period occurs during the Early Middle Ages. The term *Dark Age* doesn't refer to a specific span of years, but to the way people lived. In this context, *dark* doesn't mean "bad" or "evil." It means "silent."

What little we know of Ambrosius Aurelianus and Arthur and their battles against the Saxons comes from a Welsh monk named Gildas. In *Concerning the Ruin and Conquest of Britain* (*De excidio et conquestu Britanniae*), Gildas called Aurelianus the last of the Romans. This work, which Gildas wrote around 540 CE, is one of the few written stories we have from the Dark Ages.

When the Saxons left the island to regroup, Aurelianus acted. He launched an attack against the Saxon villages in the south—the ones Vortigern had given to the Saxons a few decades before. According to tradition, Aurelianus waged twelve battles against the Saxons.

He fought the final and most famous battle sometime between 490 and 517 CE at Mount Badon. The Saxons surrounded the Britons in the north and cut off their supply routes. Despite the disadvantage, the Britons outlasted the Saxons. When the Saxons finally withdrew, the Britons attacked them from behind and defeated them.

The legend of Arthur rose from this bloodstained battlefield at Mount Badon. He, and not Aurelianus, is credited with this victory. The defeat was so devastating that the Saxons left the island for over four decades. After generations of bloodshed, the Britons joined forces in peace. It is not hard to imagine why they kept Arthur's story alive.

Gildas never actually mentions Arthur by name as the commander who won the battle. Gildas, who was a monk, didn't care about the individual characters in his drama. He wasn't trying to write a history for future scholars to study. He just wanted to scare everyone into behaving themselves. He was warning the Britons that their evil lives would lead to their downfall.

There are very few written stories from this time period, so it is difficult to prove, without a doubt, that a man named Arthur really united the Britons. It is not surprising that so few written stories

The Britons finally defeated the Saxons at the Battle of Mount Badon. It took a strong and courageous leader to unite the British tribes against such a ruthless and formidable enemy as the Saxons.

exist. The island was constantly at war. It is unlikely that anyone had the time to write about events in a diary or a book.

During the peace that followed, something interesting happened. Both the Celts and the Britons began to name their young sons Arthur. This is important because Arthur is a Roman name, and the Romans were gone by this time. As noted by historian Geoffrey Ashe:

> In the decades after 550, despite the general vanishing of Roman names, at least four Arthurs are on record in the princely houses in Wales and Scotland. Such an out-of-line choice by at least four sets of parents, a long way apart, points to a common inspiration at work—the widespread fame of a prototype living somewhat before: a man after whom it was natural, patriotic perhaps, to name boys.[1]

By the seventh century, there were more written stories about Arthur. One of the most important written accounts is in *The Gododdin* (*Y Gododdin*) by Aneirin. According to tradition, all the warriors of

Manaw Gododdin died at the battle of Catraeth in 600 CE. The work is actually a collection of ninety-nine poems, known as elegies, dedicated to the men of Gododdin. These men lived in southeast Scotland during Arthur's time. One of Aneirin's poems champions a fallen warrior and compares him to Arthur: ". . . he fed black ravens on the ramparts, although he was no Arthur."[2]

The phrase "although he was no Arthur" suggests a character of great reputation. More important, we know that the men and events in Aneirin's poems are real. That means that most likely, the Arthur in Aneirin's poem was also real.

Two centuries after Aneirin, a Welsh monk named Nennius wrote *History of the Britons* (*Historia Brittonum*). He mentions Arthur briefly by name, but doesn't describe him as a king. Rather, he refers to him as *dux bellorum*, which means "leader of battles." He writes of the twelve battles that Arthur supposedly led. These battles are the same ones referred to by Gildas, who never mentions Arthur. Interestingly, Nennius never mentions Aurelianus. The monk credits Arthur with the victory at Mount Badon: "The twelfth battle was on Mount Badon, in which nine hundred and sixty men fell in one day from one charge by Arthur, and no one overthrew them except himself alone."[3]

Nennius adds a sorcerer, but he doesn't give him a name. The new character's mother is human; his father is a demon. Right away, it is clear that at least part of his story is fiction, either to make a point or to enhance the telling of it. Nennius also gives the boy the gift of prophecy. After seeing the future, the unnamed prophet tries to encourage the Britons by telling them that Arthur will return some day.

The most likely source for Nennius's work is Welsh stories and traditions, passed down through generations.

Despite the lack of written stories, Athur's story survived for four centuries. In fact, it more than survived: Arthur's story took on a life of its own. By the end of the Dark Ages, Arthur was a legend, but it was a legend bound to history.

The Dark Ages—
The Non-
Information Age

Many refer to the twenty-first century as the Information Age because people have such easy access to information on so many subjects. Historians in the next century and beyond should have no trouble studying people in this one. The same isn't true of earlier times, and especially not for the Dark Ages.

Francesco Petrarch

Italian scholar and poet Francesco Petrarch (1304–1374) was probably the first to use the phrase *Dark Age*. He described the men of his own age as still living in darkness and gloom, claiming the scholars and inventors of his century weren't original thinkers. In comparison to the classical Greeks and Romans, he didn't find his fellow man very innovative or even interesting.

His term was so effective that it is still used today. Academically, people still don't view the Dark Ages as a time of enlightenment. In films and books, the term refers to a time less civilized than the present. The real culprit of the time wasn't society's behavior, but rather the society's failure to write about their lives. Most people then were illiterate—they could neither read nor write.

During the Dark Ages, people kept their past alive by telling stories. For several generations, the Britons made sure their children knew of the great King Arthur, who brought peace to their savage island. Because of their tradition, the stories of King Arthur outlived the Dark Ages.

Relation	Name	Source
Arthur's wife	Ganhumara	Geoffrey
	Guinevere	Wace
variations	*Guenevere, Guenievre, Guenhumare, Ginevra, Gwenhwyfar*	
Arthur's son, nephew	Medreut/Medraut	*Annals of Wales*
	Modred	Geoffrey
	Mordred	Malory
variations	*Medrawd*	
Arthur's mother	Ygerna	Historical
	Igraine	Geoffrey
Mordred's mother	Morgan	Gerald
as Arthur's half sister	Morgan le Fay	Layamon
variations	*Morgana, Morgaine*	
Wizard	*Unnamed*	Nennius
	Merlin	Geoffrey
variations	*Merlin, Myrddin, Merlyn*	
Lady of the Lake	*Unnamed*	Historical
	Nimue	Geoffrey
	Nimue, Vivien	Malory
variations	*Viviane, Niniane, Nyneve*	

The characters in the Arthur legend change from writer to writer and century to century. Even the way the authors spelled the characters' names changed from version to version.

CHAPTER
THREE

INTO THE MIDDLE AGES

Some believe Arthur is a myth. Even during medieval times, people doubted that Arthur was a real person. The absence of an acknowledged grave or even a monument to him makes the mystery even more compelling. If Arthur existed, his story is very different from the modern tale that we enjoy today.

There are a number of opinions as to who the real Arthur might have been. Perhaps the most popular candidate is Ambrosius Aurelianus—the Roman who won several important battles against the Saxons, including the Battle of Mount Badon. Others believe he was Lucius Artorius Castus, a Roman during the second century. Some go so far as to place Arthur during the Early Bronze Age, around 2300 BCE. They base this conclusion on the sword in the stone legend. That story tells how Arthur, as a young squire, pulls a sword from a stone and therefore is proclaimed king. This story, some believe, is a metaphor for casting iron from ore (stone) in a mold and then hammering it into shape on an anvil.

Most scholars think the Arthurian legend began with Aurelianus. Four centuries after his death (around 538 CE), people were still telling his story, which was mostly still in sync with history.

The Battle of Hastings, where William the Conqueror defeated King Harold, changed Arthur's story. Geoffrey, a Norman, in an effort to flatter the conquering Normans, made the ancient King Arthur and his warriors almost indestructible.

That brings us to Geoffrey of Monmouth, a cleric and historian who wrote *History of the Kings of Britain* (*Historia regum Britanniae*) around 1137 CE. His history begins in 1200 BCE and spans two thousand years. While his stories finally give us a written record of Britain's kings, he did not base them on facts. With Geoffrey's help, the Arthur stories make a huge leap into fiction.

Geoffrey was a Norman. The duke of Normandy (modern-day France), William the Conqueror, defeated King Harold at the Battle of Hastings in 1066. Geoffrey's real motive for writing the history was to flatter and please the Norman aristocracy—the mightier he made the Britons, the stronger the conquering Normans seemed.

Geoffrey devoted half of his work to Arthur. In fact, he was probably the first to give us a complete look at Arthur's life.

Unfortunately, Geoffrey's Arthur is mostly fiction. He claims to have used an ancient text, written by Merlin, as his primary source. Historians have found no evidence that such a text ever existed. That doesn't mean that Geoffrey didn't work from an existing volume of stories. However, there's no way to know what that volume was.

The one truth we get from Geoffrey's work is that he was a great storyteller. He's the first known source to add Uther, Igraine (Ygerna), and Merlin and his magic to the story. According to Geoffrey, Uther Pendragon makes a tense peace with Gorlois, the Duke of Cornwall. During a celebration feast, Uther sees Igraine, Gorlois's wife. Uther falls madly in love with her. That's where Merlin enters the story. He's more than a prophet, he's a wizard. Under Merlin's spell, Igraine believes Uther to be her husband. Soon after, Gorlois dies in battle.

Igraine gives birth to Uther's son, Arthur, and they live at Tintagel Castle. Because this real castle was built during Geoffrey's time, it seemed unlikely that this tale could be true. However, C. A. Ralegh Radford, an archaeologist, found pottery, evidence of a fifth-century household, in the area. He concludes:

> Somewhere hereabouts a wealthy household flourished at a date corresponding to the pottery and perhaps a little before—that is, in more or less "Arthurian" times.[1]

Dated pottery doesn't prove Arthur ever lived at Tintagel Castle. It does prove that a noble family, similar to one Arthur would have belonged to, did live in that area at the right time in history.

Eventually, Uther marries Igraine and they raise Arthur together. When Uther dies, Arthur, just barely fifteen, becomes king. As a young adult, Arthur leads three important battles against the Saxons. The last takes place at Mount Badon.

Geoffrey's story shares many similarities with the factual story of Aurelianus and Arthur. Aurelianus is Uther. Insert a magician, who

Nimue, the Lady of the Lake, gives King Arthur a magic sword. Early texts mention a sword named Caliburn. Eventually, this story evolved into the story of Excalibur and its watery origin.

casts a spell upon Gorlois's faithful wife, and you get Arthur—Uther's illegitimate son. According to modern historians, the real Arthur was not Aurelianus' son; he was his stepson.

Arthur's sword, called Caliburn in this story, is more of Geoffrey's fiction. According to Geoffrey, Arthur killed 470 Saxons in a single battle with Caliburn. It's possible that the real Arthur really did kill several hundred men, but if his sword had a name, it didn't make it out of the Dark Ages. It's easy to see how the name Caliburn might have evolved into Excalibur, the magical sword in later King Arthur legends.

After defeating the Saxons, Arthur marries Ganhumara, a beautiful noble from a Roman family. After several years of peace, Rome demands money from King Arthur, which he refuses to pay. He

Guinevere, King Arthur's wife, was young and beautiful. Later authors would make her so devastatingly beautiful that the pious and loyal Sir Lancelot could not help but love her.

travels to Rome to confront the Romans, but he never makes it. During the trip, Arthur receives word from home that his nephew, Modred (whose name is sometimes spelled Mordred, Medrawd, or Medraut), has crowned himself king and forced Ganhumara into marriage—with Arthur still well and alive! Arthur hurries home and kills Modred in battle. Sadly for Geoffrey's readers, Arthur is also wounded. Like most fictional bad guys, Modred doesn't die right away. He lives just long enough to thrust his own sword into Arthur's belly. Then, Modred dies. Supposedly, Arthur recovers from his wounds on the Isle of Avalon.

Geoffrey probably got the idea for Modred and the final battle from *The Annals of Wales* (*Annales Cambriae*), which was written by Welsh monks. The *Annals* mentions Medreut, one of Arthur's warriors, who dies at the Battle of Camlann. Although Medreut starts out as Arthur's ally, later writers portray him as Arthur's nephew or son. The *Annals* does not mention any family relationship between the two men. Geoffrey probably turned Medreut, Arthur's friend, into Arthur's son and murderer, Modred. Having a relation kill the mighty King Arthur was a dramatic strategy.

Like Nennius, Geoffrey includes a wizard, but Geoffrey gives him a name: Merlin. Vortigern meets Merlin as a boy. Merlin appears in other works by Geoffrey, not just the *History of the Kings of Britain.* In the poem *The Life of Merlin* (*Vita Merlini*), Merlin goes mad after Arthur's death. Once he recovers, Merlin predicts that Arthur will return to lead Britain again. Celts, in particular the Welsh, clung to this story for centuries.

One possible source for Merlin is *The Lailoken* fragments. The collection tells the story of a wild man named Lailoken. Like Merlin, Lailoken goes mad after witnessing a horrible battle. Both men also have the gift of prophecy.

Geoffrey's contemporaries tell stories of real events and people, but they threw in magic, heroic deeds, and even miracles. Nennius credits Arthur with two miracles. In the first, a mound of stones always pushes one specific stone to the top. That stone bears the paw print of Arthur's dog, Cabal. People move the stone to the bottom of the pile, but the stone always makes its way to the top. The second miracle concerns the grave of Arthur's son, Anir. The mound of earth that covers the grave constantly changes size. By adding these two miraculous stories, Nennius transforms Arthur from a mere man into a saint.

Early Celts were a superstitious people who believed in magic. Even after the Romans introduced Christianity to the island, the Celts continued to use magic to explain the good and bad in their lives. It's easy to imagine that, given their nature, the Celts took Geoffrey's stories seriously.

Geoffrey of Monmouth

Geoffrey of Monmouth lived from 1100 to 1154 in a town called Monmouth in southeastern Wales. He was the first to tell a complete story of Arthur's life and death in a book he called *The History of the Kings of Britain* (*Historia Regum Britanniae*).

Geoffrey spent over twenty years at Oxford, England's first university. There, he wrote and taught, but he loved writing. He was teaching at Oxford when he wrote his huge volume on the British kings.

According to Geoffrey, Walter of Oxford, the provost of the college, shared an ancient Welsh document that told Arthur's story. No such book or text has ever been discovered. Since so much of Geoffrey's story is fiction, we might even doubt that such a document ever existed.

A modern photograph of Oxford University

While we can't credit Geoffrey with giving us all the historical facts we need to prove Arthur's existence, we can credit him with keeping the story alive. His work was certainly popular during his own lifetime. In fact, it was a best seller during his day.

Toward the end of his life, Geoffrey only wanted to write. He was tired of teaching. During the Middle Ages, the Catholic Church was the largest and the most powerful institution. In 1152, Geoffrey left the university and joined the church to become a priest. There, he was free to write as much as he liked.

The Order of the Round Table included King Arthur's best knights. Tradition tells us that Guinevere inherited the table from her father. Later authors would use it to introduce Christian principles into the story.

CHAPTER
FOUR

MEDIEVAL ARTHUR—
THE ROMANTIC VERSION

The next step in the Arthur legend's evolution was taken in France. In 1155, a Norman known as Wace translated Geoffrey's Latin text into French. Before, only educated nobles, monks, and priests could read the stories because they were written in Latin. Most Europeans could read French, so after Wace's translation, Arthur was suddenly available to a much larger audience.

Wace named his volume *Romance of Brutus*, and changed the story a lot. Most significantly, Wace introduced the Round Table. With no head, no knight sitting at the table could claim superiority over any other. Wace was also the first to add love to Arthur's story— although he admitted that some of the stories weren't true:

> The tales of Arthur are not all lies nor are they true.
> So much have the story-tellers told and so much have
> the makers of fables fabled to embellish their stories
> that they have made everything seem a fable.[1]

A British priest named Layamon doubled the length of the story when he translated Wace's work into English. Women dressed in black don't save King Arthur after the final battle; fairies whisk him away. There, his half sister, Morgan le Fay, heals his wounds using magic. While Layamon did not keep to facts, he certainly was creative.

Although inventive, Layamon's version is gloomy. Arthur's knights are often enemies. Arthur dreams that Modred and Guinevere betray him. While sitting on the roof of the hall, Arthur begins to chop the pillars that support the roof. Guinevere then pulls down the roof and Arthur falls to the ground. In the fall, he breaks his arm, but he also cuts off Modred's head. Then he hacks Guinevere to bits.

Wace's version was more wholesome than Layamon's. His knights were often rivals, but never enemies. His mix was just right for the time, and his version became extremely popular throughout Europe.

With Henry II's encouragement, other writers took Wace's stories even further. Henry went so far as to claim he was an ancestor of Arthur's, trying to legitimize his claim to the crown. He also used Arthur's stories to promote the idea of British superiority. During medieval days, these stories became known as the Matter of Britain. (In those days, bards told three types of stories: the Matter of Britain, the Matter of Rome, and the Matter of France.)

Henry wasn't alone in using the King Arthur stories. His wife, Eleanor of Aquitaine, used Arthur to promote ideals of courtly love. She paid writers to add romantic love stories to the existing legends. The real nobles and knights weren't at war, so they needed something to do. Reading about courtly love was just one of the ways they entertained themselves. In these stories, a knight chose a noble lady, usually a married one, to love from afar. He devoted himself to her pleasures and needs and protected her. In return, he received nothing but honor.

It's important to set the record straight about chivalry and courtly love. These virtuous knights didn't exist in any kingly court—they were just stories. Courtly love, chivalry, and all the other romantic ideals from this era are fluff. Men and women probably fell in love, but the only knights loving virtuous ladies from afar lived in stories.

The medieval Arthur was nothing like the real fifth-century Arthur. During this era, King Arthur was no longer the regal and noble king of the early Middle Ages who united Britain. Later readers no longer needed the warrior king. They turned him into a victim of love and betrayal. They wanted a righteous, vulnerable, and chivalrous king.

Chrétien de Troyes was one of the medieval writers who complicated Arthur's life with courtly love. Eleanor's daughter, the Countess Marie de Champagne, hired him to produce romantic stories based on King Arthur and his knights. Readers wanted stories of unobtainable love and betrayal, and that's what he gave them. Chrétien introduced the love affair between Lancelot and Guinevere. This affair of the heart is pure fiction and was meant to please his romantic readers—especially the countess.

Another Chrétien addition is Camelot, the site of Arthur's castle. Historians believe Chrétien used the short form of *Camulodunum*, a Roman name for the city of Colchester.

Excavation in 1966 at another possible site for Camelot, Cadbury Castle, uncovered a fort large enough to house one thousand troops. This discovery doesn't prove that Arthur was ever there. However, the excavated gate tower, great hall, and fort are consistent with the stories.

Medieval Arthur sees two more significant changes. Some writers began to push a Christian theme using the Round Table and the Holy Grail.

In the beginning, the Round Table was exactly what one might think—a piece of furniture. Its roundness eased the competitive and often volatile nature of Arthur's knights. At a round table, all the knights were equal.

The Holy Grail was the cup of Jesus at the Last Supper. Some claimed Mary used it to catch her son's blood as he died on the cross. According to legend, only the pure of heart could see the Holy Grail. King Arthur's knights had many adventures trying to find it. Sir Galahad (Lancelot's son by Lady Elaine) was the only knight pure enough to succeed. Shortly after seeing the Grail, he died.

Tradition claims that this table, which hangs in Winchester Castle, is King Arthur's Round Table. However, tree-ring and radiocarbon dating reveal that the table was constructed around 1270, near the beginning of King Edward I's reign. The names of King Arthur's knights inscribed on the table are Sirs Galahad, Lancelot du Lac, Gawain, Percivale, Lionell, Tristram de Lyones, Gareth, Bedivere, Bleoberis, La Cote Male Taile, Lucan, Palomedes, Lamorak, Bors de Ganis, Safer, Pelleas, Kay, Ector de Maris, Dagonet, Degore, Brunor le Noir, Le Bel Desconneu, Alymere, and Mordred.

The actual object is insignificant. The Grail is symbolic and represents the link between the sacred and the ordinary. It reminds us that there are better things beyond the mortal lives we lead. The secret of the Grail is simple—it is knowledge.

Most likely, the legend of the Grail got its start from a Welsh poem from the tenth or eleventh century. According to the poem,

Arthur stole a magic pot during a raid into Wales. The pot wouldn't cook for a coward. Over the years, this coward-exposing cauldron may have evolved into the legendary Holy Grail.

The cauldron comes from a sixth-century story told by Taliesin, a bard. This poem mentions Arthur, a warrior and not a king, by name. He and his men journey to the Otherworld to find a magical vessel. The Grail doesn't appear again until Chrétien writes *Perceval,* or *The Story of the Grail* (*Le Conte del Graal*) in the late twelfth century. He failed to finish the poem, which added to the Grail's mystery.

During the Crusades of the twelfth century, a French poet named Robert de Borron linked the Round Table and the Holy Grail to an early tradition that claimed that Jesus and his apostles ate the Last Supper at the Round Table. It's possible that knights returning from the Crusades in the Holy Lands brought the medieval version of the Grail with them when they returned. However, this later version only enhances the Grail story—it existed in legend long before the Crusades.

According to the medieval version, the Holy Grail, the cup from which Jesus drank at the Last Supper, was passed to Joseph of Arimathea, the man who removed the body of Jesus from the cross. Most likely, Joseph was Jesus' uncle.

Hoping to spread Christianity, Joseph traveled to the British Isles in 63 CE, and he took the Holy Grail with him. During the journey, Joseph and his group reenacted the Last Supper at a table they called the Grail Table.

Once in Britain, Joseph met Uther Pendragon, who built his own Grail Table and called it the Round Table. When he died, the table passed to Guinevere's father.

Not only did Borron twist the story of the Round Table to support Christian principles, he switched the focus of the stories from King Arthur to his knights and their Order of the Round Table.

As for the Holy Grail, the story has Joseph bury it near the abbey for safekeeping. Later, in the nineteenth century, the story evolves even more. According to tradition, water bubbled up from the spot where Joseph had buried the Holy Grail, feeding a new spring. A well, known as the Chalice Well, now marks the spot. Supposedly, the water in the well occasionally has a red tint.

Today, we credit Sir Thomas Malory with changing Arthur the most, and not for the better. Malory turns Arthur into a betrayed husband and monarch. Like so often in this journey, the changes are all fiction.

In *Morte D'Arthur* (*The Death of Arthur*), written around 1470, Malory doesn't specify a time period for Arthur's adventures, but his settings place Arthur during medieval times. His knights wear metal full-body armor and challenge one another in tournaments. In their spare time, they show their devotion to fair maidens without hope of ever winning their hearts.

Magic, the supernatural, and superstition have always been part of the Arthurian tradition. Malory's Arthur is so full of all three that the original Arthur is barely recognizable.

Tradition has held that Excalibur, King Arthur's sword, protected him through some mystical power. Malory's Arthur finds himself without a sword, having broken his in battle. Merlin leads the king to a lake near Camelot. Arthur's eyes follow Merlin's outstretched arm as he points to the middle of the lake. From the still, clear water, King Arthur watches a lady's arm break the surface. In her hand, Nimue, the Lady of the Lake, holds a sword. She agrees to give King Arthur the sword. In return, King Arthur agrees to grant her a favor whenever she asks. Wielding Excalibur, King Arthur can never be defeated, but the real magic is in the sword's silver scabbard. As long as he wears the scabbard, he can't die.

While in London's Newgate Prison, Malory spun his version of Sir Lancelot and Queen Guinevere, in which Lancelot, for love of Guinevere, destroys the Order of the Round Table and kills Arthur.

Medieval knights competed in jousting matches. Most modern legends place King Arthur and his knights during the medieval period of knights, chivalry, and courtly love and intrigue.

Most likely, Malory lifted his Lancelot from *Prose Lancelot*, written between 1215 and 1230. (This story was part of a larger volume named the *Vulgate Cycle*.) Malory's Lancelot is the most righteous of all the knights, and King Arthur loves Lancelot the best. Lancelot is the strongest in battle, but weak where Guinevere is concerned. Malory's Queen Guinevere and Sir Lancelot fall in love. Although the two remain loyal to Arthur, everyone at court knows they love one another—everyone, that is, but Arthur. Many are jealous of Arthur's devotion to Guinevere, so she is an easy target for a murderous plot.

While Lancelot recovers from a wound in a faraway kingdom, Guinevere unknowingly offers a piece of poisoned fruit to a knight. He eats the fruit and dies immediately. His brother accuses Guinevere of murdering the knight, and he demands justice.

According to the law, the only way Guinevere can prove her innocence is for someone to defeat the accusing knight in battle.

Not one knight steps forward to defend her honor. Just in time, Lancelot shows up and defeats the dead knight's brother. Guinevere is declared innocent of the charge.

Soon there is more treachery. Guinevere is found guilty of treason against the king and the court sentences her to death. Of course, Lancelot saves her, but Camelot falls into civil war. Guinevere, Lancelot, and King Arthur do not live happily ever after.

There were no knights in the fifth century, only warriors and soldiers. Knights did not come along until much later. Arthur's fifth-century warriors did not wear metal full-body armor, and they did not practice at tournaments. They were too busy fighting real battles. Most importantly, chivalry was the invention of medieval writers. Malory's Arthur has almost no resemblance to the real Arthur of the fifth century.

Malory's Merlin is also different and comes to a tragic end. Merlin's favorite student, Vivien (who is sometimes called Nimue, the Lady of the Lake), betrays him. She sings an enchanting song to lull him to sleep. Then she imprisons him in a tower of air. According to Malory, Merlin is still trapped in Vivien's tower, waiting to be released.

Malory transforms one of the story's main, and most interesting, villains, Morgan le Fay. In earlier versions, Morgan plays many roles. Most often she is Arthur's half sister. In the most sinister versions, she is also Mordred's mother and Gorlois' daughter. To avenge her father's death, she must destroy Arthur. Using magic, she conceives Arthur's child. She raises the boy, Mordred, on hate for his father. She tucks him in at night with horrific scenes of death and mayhem—the price he will exact from Arthur when he is a grown man.

Malory's Morgan remains a magical being (*fay* means "fairy"), but she is one of good and healing. It is Morgan who retrieves the dying Arthur and takes him to the Isle of Avalon, where she heals him.

Sir Thomas Malory, the Knight Prisoner

Sir Thomas Malory penned the most romantic version of King Arthur and his knights. As a man, Malory is almost as much a mystery as the King Arthur he made so popular. He was born into a gentry family in Warwickshire, England, in or near 1416. As an adult, he owned land, married, had a son, and even held political office. By 1441, he was a knight. Despite all these advantages and achievements, he became a notorious criminal.

A page from Thomas Malory's Morte d'Arthur

During 1450 he supposedly committed a number of serious crimes, including assault, extortion, and theft. Historians aren't absolutely certain that the author Malory, of King Arthur fame, is the same Sir Thomas Malory who was a knight, criminal, and prisoner. However, most agree that they are probably the same person.

By January 1452, Malory was living in prison, where he spent most of the next eight years. Early during his captivity, he got out on bail a couple of times. He couldn't behave himself, and each time the authorities sent him back to prison. Once he even escaped by using a sword and a lot of drama. The authorities recaptured him and sent him back to prison. However, they moved him around a lot. By moving him around, they hoped to keep him from making friends with the caretakers and guards and escaping again. No court ever tried or convicted him during those eight years.

Malory wrote most of his Arthur stories while in prison. He wrote them in English and called them *The Book of King Arthur and His Noble Knights of the Round Table*. There are eight tales in a total of twenty-one books. When William Caxton printed the work in 1485, he renamed it *Morte d'Arthur* (*The Death of Arthur*).

Even today, readers find Malory's stories entertaining. However, they are of no help to historians, because they are pure fiction.

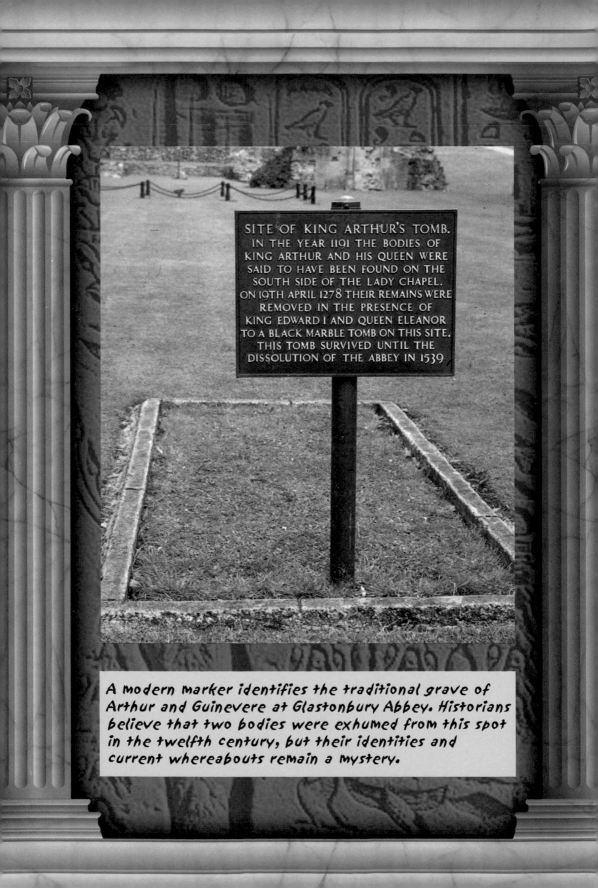

SITE OF KING ARTHUR'S TOMB.
IN THE YEAR 1191 THE BODIES OF
KING ARTHUR AND HIS QUEEN WERE
SAID TO HAVE BEEN FOUND ON THE
SOUTH SIDE OF THE LADY CHAPEL.
ON 19TH APRIL 1278 THEIR REMAINS WERE
REMOVED IN THE PRESENCE OF
KING EDWARD I AND QUEEN ELEANOR
TO A BLACK MARBLE TOMB ON THIS SITE.
THIS TOMB SURVIVED UNTIL THE
DISSOLUTION OF THE ABBEY IN 1539

A modern marker identifies the traditional grave of
Arthur and Guinevere at Glastonbury Abbey. Historians
believe that two bodies were exhumed from this spot
in the twelfth century, but their identities and
current whereabouts remain a mystery.

CHAPTER
FIVE

THE FINAL MYSTERIES— DEATH AND IDENTITY

Even Arthur's death is a mystery. Geoffrey of Monmouth was probably the first to have Modred kill Arthur—but his version is fiction. Malory had Lancelot do the dreadful deed. According to some legends, Arthur recovered from these wounds at the Isle of Avalon.

The fifth-century Arthur did die in battle around 538 CE, possibly during a civil war. We do not know where he was buried. Gerald of Wales, a churchman during the twelfth century and of noble birth, wrote of finding Arthur's grave.

In 1191, monks from Glastonbury Abbey claimed that they had found the graves of Arthur and Guinevere. According to Gerald, they found Arthur's body between two stone pyramids that had been in the churchyard for as long as anyone could remember. The stones were so old that the inscriptions on both pyramids were worn away. Buried seventeen feet deep between these two stones, Arthur's remains were found in a coffin made of a hollowed-out tree trunk. The monks also found a stone slab with a lead cross attached to its underside. On the cross was the inscription: *Here in the Isle of Avalon lies buried the renowned King Arthur, with Guinevere, his second wife.* They found Guinevere's bones at Arthur's feet. According to tradition, a monk found a strand of blond hair in the coffin, but it disintegrated when he tried to pick it up. This tidbit seems unlikely, as the hair would have disintegrated long before then.

Although abbey records supposedly left clues to Arthur's grave, no one had searched the abbey for the grave. Then, as tradition goes, a fortuneteller told King Henry II where to find Arthur's body.

Ralph of Coggeshall wrote *English Chronicle* (*Chronicon Anglicanum*), a history of England that covers 1187 to 1224. He also described Arthur's grave at Glastonbury. In his version, the monks were digging a grave for a fellow monk when they found Arthur's coffin, quite by accident. Another discrepancy between the two versions is the way they spelled *Arthur*. Gerald used the spelling *Arthurus;* Ralph used *Arturius*. The two didn't agree on where the cross was found, either. Ralph claimed the cross was placed on the coffin, not beneath the coffin as Gerald remembered.

Curiously, modern Glastonbury was called the Isle of Avalon in ancient times. Avalon is where they took Arthur to recover after he was wounded in his final battle. Glastonbury was surrounded by marshlands, and a hill rose from the center of the marshes, like an island. According to Gerald, after the Battle of Camlann, Morgan carried Arthur to the Isle of Avalon, where she nursed his wounds.

King Edward I moved the remains of Arthur and Guinevere to the abbey church in 1278. They laid Arthur's cross on top of the tomb.

C. A. Ralegh Radford excavated Glastonbury in 1962 and found proof that monks did dig up a grave at about the time Gerald and Ralph claim. However, one clue suggests that the cross might be a fake. The lettering on the only surviving drawing uses a style that dates to the tenth century. Radford suggests that Arthur was buried there, but that tenth-century monks used the cross to mark the grave. Most likely, they didn't intend to deceive anyone.

Other historians say the grave is a hoax. Supposedly, the monks were in need of money after the abbey burned in 1184. Finding Arthur's tomb was a publicity stunt to raise money.

Politics gives us the most believable version. By medieval times England had only one king. However, the Welsh continued to wait for Arthur's return, which made them a bit unruly. They believed Merlin's promise that Arthur would return to rule them once again. A crook could easily have taken advantage of the Welsh tradition and pretended to be Arthur to gain power. Some historians believe that Henry II or his son, Richard I, paid the monks of the abbey to *discover* Arthur's body as proof that Arthur was actually dead. It seems odd to us now that such an action would be necessary, but the tradition of Arthur was powerful, and in those days the Welsh were superstitious.

The graves and the cross remained in the abbey church for the next 250 years. John Leland (c. 1506–1552), a librarian to King Henry VIII, traveled throughout England. He claimed to have actually seen the cross in 1540. He drew a picture of it (the only one that survives), which was later published in the 1607 edition of *Britannia* by William Camden. Historians value Leland's works, especially his *History and Antiquities*. However, Leland eventually went insane. Whether his cross story is true is not known. There is nothing to suggest that he was mentally ill when he wrote the story.

No one knows what happened to the abbey tomb. The tomb and the remains were probably destroyed during the English Reformation. After the Pope excommunicated King Henry VIII for divorcing his first wife without papal permission, Henry started his own church—the Church of England. Most English people didn't really mind because the Catholic Church demanded money for everything: to get married, to have a child baptized, and so on. The wealthiest Catholics were monks. Henry seized the churches and monasteries and their wealth. Many churches were destroyed. According to tradition, the cross was sent to St. John the Baptist church in Glastonbury. It disappeared sometime during the eighteenth century.

The real Arthur must have been a man for all times, as the legend tells us. Remember, Nimue promised King Arthur would return someday. For now, we have to settle for stories to keep him alive.

FYI
For Your Info

Arthur's Legacy

After 1,500 years of being handed down from one generation to the next, Arthur's story is more fantasy than reality. We'll probably never know more than is known right now about the real Arthur. It is amazing that his stories still influence us, but they do.

The English royal family uses titles connected to Arthur. The prince is called the Duke of Cornwall, in memory of Arthur's birthplace. The prince receives the title of Prince of Wales at the age of fifteen because that's when Arthur became king of Britain.

Our literature, both ancient and modern, is full of Arthur's stories. Not all are strictly about Arthur, but they are based on the knights of the Round Table and the magic that influenced their lives. Several books written in the last two hundred years are about Arthur. One of the most famous is Mark Twain's *A Connecticut Yankee in King Arthur's Court.* Marion Zimmer Bradley's modern version of Arthur, *The Mists of Avalon,* was a best-selling book and popular television miniseries. Early television viewers watched *The Adventures of Sir Lancelot* each week. Even the science fiction series *Stargate SG-1* devoted a few episodes to Arthur.

Marion Zimmer Bradley

Supposedly, the movies *Star Wars* and *Indiana Jones and the Last Crusade* are based on the King Arthur stories. Disney's cartoon *The Sword in the Stone* is a children's version of the King Arthur story. *Camelot,* a Broadway play and movie, sets Malory's version of King Arthur to music.

Each year, thousands of people visit Arthurian sites throughout England. Glastonbury Abbey, where Joseph of Arimathea supposedly buried the Holy Grail and where Arthur and Guinevere may have been buried, is one favorite tourist spot. Tintagel Castle is another.

Few historical characters continue to be so popular after 1,500 years. Arthur's popularity is odd, if you consider that he was just a man who ruled Britain during the fifth century. But it's more than that. The notion that one man's deeds can be greater than the sum of his life challenges us to be better than we are.

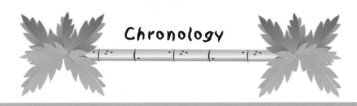

Chronology

Dates are approximate

465–475	Arthur is born.
485–496	Gildas writes of twelve battles between Arthur and the Saxons.
490	Arthur becomes king.
490–517	Arthur defeats the Saxons at the Battle of Mount Badon (Badon Hill, a fortress on Hadrian's Wall).
537–542	Arthur dies at the Battle of Camlann.
540	Gildas writes *Concerning the Ruin and Conquest of Britain (De excidio et conquestu Britanniae)*.
600	Ancirin writes *The Gododdin (Y Gododdin)*, in which he compares a fallen warrior to Arthur.
820	Nennius writes *History of the Britons (Historia Brittonum)*; historians disagree as to the true authorship of this volume.
1137	Geoffrey of Monmouth writes *History of the Kings of Britain (Historia regum Britanniae)*.
1155	Wace translates Geoffrey's Latin text into French.
1177–1181	Chrétien de Troyes romanticizes earlier versions for his patron Countess Marie de Champagne.
1191	Monks at Glastonbury Abbey claim to have found the graves of Arthur and Guinevere.
1200	Robert de Borron links the Holy Grail and the Round Table to Christian principles.
1215	Layamon doubles the length of Wace's French version while translating the story into English.
1215–1230	*Prose Lancelot*, part of a larger volume called the *Vulgate Cycle*, is written.
1278	King Edward I moves the remains of Arthur and Guinevere to the abbey church.
1470	Sir Thomas Malory writes *Morte D'Arthur (The Death of Arthur)*.
1607	William Camden publishes *Britannia*, which contains a picture of the cross believed to have been found with the remains of Arthur and Guinevere at Glastonbury Abbey.

BIOGRAPHY FROM

ANCIENT CIVILIZATIONS

LEGENDS, FOLKLORE, AND STORIES OF ANCIENT WORLDS

Timeline
in History

Dates are approximate

55 BCE	Julius Caesar invades Britain.
63 CE	Joseph of Arimathea arrives in Glastonbury on what is believed to be the first Christian mission to Britain.
75–77	Roman conquest of Britain is complete.
122	Construction on Hadrian's Wall begins.
184	Lucius Artorius Castus takes troops to Gaul to put down a rebellion; some believe Lucius is Arthur.
410	Led by Alaric, the Visigoths attack and capture Rome.
438	Ambrosius Aurelianus is born.
440–450	Civil war and famine spread through Britain after the Roman legions abandon the island and return to Rome.
445	Vortigern becomes king.
446	Vortigern hires Saxon mercenaries to help fight the Celtic tribes.
447	Welsh monks begin *The Annals of Wales (Annales Cambriae),* on which Geoffrey will later base some of his writings.
450	After years of fighting, Anglo-Saxons control parts of Britain.
457	Vortigern dies.
458–460	British nobles move to Brittany, fleeing the Saxons.
460–470	Ambrosius Aurelianus takes control of Britain and leads Britons against the Saxons; he becomes king.
476	Dark Ages begin.
490–517	The Saxons are defeated at the Battle of Mount Badon.
600	Anglo-Saxons control almost all of Britain.
1000	Dark Ages end.
1066	William the Conqueror defeats King Harold at the Battle of Hastings.
1147–1149	Second Crusade; tradition holds that English knights may have returned from the Holy Lands with the Grail.
1529–1536	The English Reformation results in the creation of the Church of England.

Further Reading and Chapter Notes

For Young Adults

Doherty, Paul C. *King Arthur*. New York: Chelsea House Publishers, 1987.

Goodrich, Norma Lorre. *Guinevere*. New York: HarperCollins Publishers, 1991.

———. *King Arthur*. New York: Franklin Watts, 1986.

Kerven, Rosalind. *King Arthur*. London: DK Publishing, Inc., 1998.

Lister, Robin. *The Legend of King Arthur*. New York: Doubleday, 1988.

O'Neal, Michael. *King Arthur: Opposing Viewpoints*. San Diego: Greenhaven Press, Inc., 1992.

Schlesinger, Arthur M., Jr. *King Arthur*. New York: Chelsea House Publishers, 1987.

Wyly, Michael J. *King Arthur*. San Diego: Lucent Books, Inc., 2001.

Works Consulted

Ashe, Geoffrey. *The Discovery of King Arthur*. New York: Anchor Press, 1985.

Blundell, Nigel, and Kate Farrington. *Ancient England*. London: Chartwell Books, Inc., 1996.

Edge, David, and John Miles Paddock. *Arms and Armor of the Medieval Knight*. New York: Crescent Books, 1988.

Hopkins, Andrea. *Knights*. New York: Shooting Star Press, Inc., 1990.

Matthews, John. *The Mystic Grail: The Challenge of the Arthurian Quest*. New York: Sterling Publishing Co., Inc., 1997.

Pyle, Howard. *The Story of the Champions of the Round Table*. New York: Charles Scribner's Sons, undated.

———. *The Story of the Grail*. New York: Charles Scribner's Sons, 1910.

Stobie, Denise. *Exploring King Arthur's Britain*. London: Collins & Brown Ltd., 1999.

On the Internet

The Camelot Project at the University of Rochester http://www.lib.rochester.edu/camelot/cphome.stm

Y Gododdin http://www.missgien.net/celtic/gododdin

King Arthur and the Knights of the Round Table http://www.kingarthursknights.com

Original sources and text related to King Arthur http://www.britannia.com/history/artdocs.html

Chapter Notes

Chapter 2. Out of the Dark Ages

1. Geoffrey Ashe, *The Discovery of King Arthur* (New York: Anchor Press, 1985), p. 78.
2. Ibid., p. 137.
3. Ibid., p. 69.

Chapter 3. Into the Middle Ages

1. Geoffrey Ashe, *The Discovery of King Arthur* (New York: Anchor Press, 1985), p. 78.

Chapter 4. Medieval Arthur—The Romantic Version

1. Geoffrey Ashe, *The Discovery of King Arthur* (New York: Anchor Press, 1985), p. 13.

Index